Your True Worth

Your True Worth

Your True Worth

By

Sweeden Peters

Acknowledgments

Dear Heavenly Father,

I come before you with a heart overflowing with gratitude. I acknowledge that every word, every idea, every moment of inspiration came from you. You are the author of this message, and I am simply the vessel you have used to bring it to light.

I thank you for the vision you planted in my heart, for the passion you fueled in my soul, and for the perseverance you granted me to see this through. I thank you for the late nights and early mornings, for the sacrifices and the challenges, knowing that they were all part of the journey you had for me.

I pray that this book will be a reflection of your unconditional love, a testament to the freedom and fulfillment found in seeking your validation alone. I pray it would be a light in the darkness, a balm to the souls of those who read it, and a catalyst for transformation in the lives of your daughters and sons.

I thank you for the people you have placed in my life to support and encourage me on this journey. For my family, whose love and sacrifice made this possible. For my friends and community, whose prayers and encouragement have been my lifeline. For my team, whose expertise and dedication have helped bring this message to the world.

I ask your continued blessing on this work, Lord. May it find its way to those you have for it, and may it bring the freedom and fulfillment you promise. May it be a tool in

Your True Worth

your hands, shaping and transforming lives for your

glory.

In the name of Jesus, I pray. Amen.

Dedication

To Shana and Emilsa,

Two women whose light doesn't just shine – it warms
and transforms all it touches.

Shana, in your quiet strength, I see a reflection of the
unshakeable rock of God's love. Your worth, dear one, is
etched into the very fabric of your being. You are
beloved, not for what you do, but for who you are – a
cherished daughter of the King.

Emilsa, your love is oxygen – it breathes life into the
souls of those around you. In your care and devotion, I
see the heartbeat of our Heavenly Father. You are seen,
you are valued, you are vital. Your presence matters
more than you may ever know.

May you both walk in the freedom that comes from
knowing your true worth. Seek validation only from the
One who made you, who adores you just as you are.
Shine His light, dear ones, and watch as your lives
become a testament to His power to transform and
redeem.

With tears of admiration and gratitude,

Sweeden

Your True Worth

Your True Worth

Table of Content

Part 1: The Trap of Seeking Human Validation

Part 2: Finding True Validation in God's Word

Your True Worth

Your True Worth

Part 1:

The Trap of Seeking Human Validation

Introduction

I still remember the day it hit me – the crushing realization that no matter how hard I tried, I could never earn the approval of everyone around me. I was caught in a relentless cycle, constantly striving to meet the expectations of my friends, family, even strangers on social media. At work, I poured myself into project after project, thinking the next promotion would finally bring the validation I craved. But the more I sought validation from the world, the emptier I felt.

Perhaps you know this struggle all too well. In a society that screams for our attention with likes, shares, and followers, it's easy to fall into the trap of believing our worth is tied to human approval. We chase success, thinking the next achievement will finally bring the

Your True Worth

validation we crave. We compare our lives to the highlight reels of others, feeling inadequate and unnoticed. At work, we sacrifice boundaries and burn out in an attempt to prove our value. But the truth is, this relentless pursuit of people-pleasing will leave us perpetually drained and discontent.

As a psychology student, I delved deep into the human mind, studying why we crave validation and how it shapes our behavior. But it wasn't until I integrated the teachings of my Christian upbringing that everything clicked into place. I realized that our deepest longing for approval is ultimately a longing for God's unconditional love and acceptance.

This book is an invitation to leave the exhausting hunt for human approval behind and discover the transformative power of seeking God's validation above all else. Through personal stories, biblical teachings, and practical wisdom, we'll explore what it means to find our identity and worth in the eyes of God alone – both in our personal lives and in our careers. Get ready to experience the freedom that comes when you stop chasing the fleeting praise of people and start living for the eternal approval of your Creator. Because in the end, God's validation is the only one that truly matters.

Now that we've seen the struggle of seeking human validation, let's turn our attention to the freedom that comes from seeking God's approval instead. In the following chapters, we'll delve into what it means to find our worth in His unconditional love, and how this transforms every area of our lives.

Your True Worth

Chapter 1: The World's Expectations

vs. God's Expectations

"Do not conform to the pattern of this world, but be transformed by the renewing of your mind. Then you will be able to test and approve what God's will is—his good, pleasing and perfect will." - Romans 12:2

The world has a never-ending list of expectations for us. From the moment we wake up until we collapse into bed at night, we're bombarded with messages telling us how to live, what to achieve, and who to be. Social media screams for our attention, whispering lies that our worth is tied to our likes and followers. Advertisements promise that if we just buy this product or that service, we'll finally be enough. At work, we're often measured

Your True Worth

by our productivity and success, with the implication that our value comes from what we can produce.

This pressure to constantly perform is exhausting. We feel like we're on a treadmill that's spinning out of control. No matter how hard we run, we can't seem to get ahead. And the more we strive to meet the world's expectations, the emptier we feel. We start to lose touch with who we truly are and what we deeply desire.

But here's the beautiful thing: God's expectations are radically different. He doesn't expect us to earn His approval. He doesn't measure our worth by our achievements or our appearance. He doesn't compare us to others or demand that we fit into a certain mold. Instead, He loves us as we are, right now. He sees our messy, imperfect selves and says, "You are enough. You are beloved. You are Mine."

This is the freedom that comes from seeking God's expectations instead of the world's. When we anchor our identity in His unconditional love, we're no longer slaves to the endless expectations of others. We're free to live the life He designed for us, to pursue the purposes He placed on our hearts. In the following chapters, we'll dive deeper into what it means to live according to God's expectations, not the world's. We'll explore how to break free from the cycle of people-pleasing and find true validation in our Heavenly Father's approval. But for now, take a moment to reflect on the expectations that have been driving your life. Are you trying to earn approval from the world, or are you seeking the unconditional love of God?

Chapter 2: The Never-Ending Cycle of People-Pleasing

"Am I now trying to win the approval of human beings, or of God? Or am I trying to please people? If I were still trying to please people, I would not be a servant of Christ." - Galatians 1:10

People-pleasing is an exhausting game. It's a never-ending cycle of trying to meet the expectations of others, of constantly striving to earn their approval and validation. We say yes to requests we don't have time for, not wanting to disappoint others even if it means sacrificing our own needs. We mold ourselves into who we think others want us to be, hiding our true selves in fear of rejection. We work tirelessly to prove our worth, as if our value is tied to our achievements and successes.

Your True Worth

But here's the brutal truth: we can never please everyone. No matter how hard we try, there will always be someone who disapproves, someone who expects more, someone who tells us we're not enough. And when we anchor our worth in the shifting sands of human approval, we'll forever be chasing a validation that remains just out of reach.

I know this cycle all too well. For years, I found myself constantly trying to please those around me. I took on projects at work that drained me, not wanting to let my team down. I agreed to social plans even when I craved quiet, fearing that saying no would lead to rejection. I sacrificed my own needs and desires, molding myself into who I thought others wanted me to be.

Your True Worth

But the more I people-pleased, the emptier I felt. I was like a shell of myself, devoid of the passions and interests that once brought me joy. I felt like I was living someone else's life, not my own. And through it all, I was still haunted by the fear of not being enough.

It wasn't until I hit rock bottom, burnt out and depleted, that I realized the destructive nature of people-pleasing. I saw that in my relentless pursuit of human approval, I had lost myself. I had forgotten what it meant to live a life that was pleasing to God, not others.

In the following chapters, we'll explore how to break free from the cycle of people-pleasing and find true validation in God's unconditional love. We'll learn what it means to be a servant of Christ, not a slave to the expectations of others. But for now, take a moment to

Your True Worth

reflect on your own tendencies towards people-pleasing. Where are you sacrificing your own needs and desires in an attempt to earn the approval of others? What would it look like to live a life that is pleasing to God, even if that means disappointing others?

Chapter 3: The Emptiness of Validation

Through Material Success

"For where your treasure is, there your heart will be also." - Matthew 6:21

In our culture, success is often measured by what we can see. The size of our house, the brand of our car, the number in our bank account – these are the metrics that scream "You've made it!" But validation through material success is fleeting at best and damaging at worst.

Perhaps you know the feeling. You land the promotion you've been working towards, and for a moment, you feel like you're on top of the world. You buy the house and the car and the fancy clothes, thinking that if you

Your True Worth

look successful, you'll feel successful. But as time goes on, that initial high wears off, leaving you feeling empty and unfulfilled. No matter how hard you work, you can't shake the feeling that you're always one step away from failure.

This is the danger of tying our worth to our achievements. When we define ourselves by our success, we're building our identity on shaky ground. We become like hamsters on a wheel, constantly running but getting nowhere. We sacrifice our health and our relationships in an attempt to prove ourselves, all while feeling lost and unfulfilled deep down.

And then, when those achievements are taken away, we're left with nothing. We're forced to confront the emptiness we've been trying to fill with success and

Your True Worth

status. This can be a painful realization, but it can also be a chance to rebuild our identity on a firmer foundation.

In the following chapters, we'll explore what it means to find our worth in God's eyes, not in our accomplishments. We'll learn to define ourselves by His unconditional love, not by the fleeting validation of the world. But for now, take a moment to reflect on where you're seeking validation through material success. What would happen to your sense of self if those achievements were taken away? Where can you begin to shift your focus from earthly treasures to eternal ones?

Chapter 4: The Danger of Comparison

"Therefore, I do not run like someone running aimlessly; I do not fight like one punching the air. Rather, I discipline my body and bring it under strict control so that, after I have preached to others, I myself will not be disqualified." - 1 Corinthians 9:26-27

Comparison is a dangerous game. It's a slippery slope that can lead us down a path of discontentment, jealousy, and a never-ending cycle of striving to be someone we're not. We look at the highlight reels of others, comparing our behind-the-scenes to their carefully curated moments of success. We measure our worth by the metrics of the world, feeling like we fall short when we don't stack up.

Your True Worth

But here's the thing: comparison robs us of joy. It keeps us focused on what we lack, rather than what we have. It fuels our insecurities and feeds our fears. And perhaps most damaging, comparison keeps us from being the person God created us to be. When we're too busy looking at others, we miss the unique purpose and calling that's ours alone.

The apostle Paul understood this. He knew that his race, his fight, was unique to him. He wasn't running aimlessly, comparing himself to others, but instead, he was focused on his own journey of faith. He disciplined his body and brought it under control, not to earn the approval of others, but to stay the course of his calling.

This is a powerful lesson for us. In a world that screams for our attention, it's easy to get caught up in comparison. But when we do, we risk being disqualified from the very purpose God has for us. We risk living someone else's life, rather than the one He designed for us.

So how can we break the cycle of comparison? How can we stay focused on our own race, our own fight?

Here are a few practical steps:

- Turn your eyes upon Jesus. In times of comparison, bring your focus back to Him. Seek His truth and His approval, not the fleeting validation of the world.
- Celebrate others' successes. When you feel the urge to compare, choose to cheer on those around you instead. Their wins are not your losses.

Your True Worth

- Embrace your uniqueness. You are uniquely wired with gifts and talents that no one else possesses. Embrace what makes you different, rather than trying to be someone you're not.

- Set boundaries with social media. If comparison is a struggle for you, it may be wise to limit your time on platforms that fuel this cycle.

Comparison is a dangerous game, but it's one we can overcome. By keeping our eyes on Jesus, celebrating others, embracing our uniqueness, and setting healthy boundaries, we can break the cycle of comparison and live the life God designed for us.

Take a moment to reflect on where comparison is stealing your joy. Where are you looking at others, rather than focusing on your own journey? What steps can you

Your True Worth

take to break the cycle of comparison and stay the course
of your unique calling?

Part 2

Finding True Validation in God's Word

Chapter 5: God's Unconditional Love and Acceptance

"And so we know and rely on the love God has for us. God is love. Whoever lives in love lives in God, and God in them." - 1 John 4:16

The world's love is conditional. It says, "I'll love you if..." If you perform well enough, if you look a certain way, if you achieve great things. But this kind of love is fleeting, always just out of reach. No matter how hard we try, we can never quite earn the unconditional approval of others.

But God's love is different. His love is not based on our performance or our appearance. It's not something we have to earn or strive for. Instead, God's love is

Your True Worth

unconditional, a gift freely given to us simply because we exist. He loves us in our messiness, in our brokenness, in our imperfectness. He sees us as we are, and He says, "You are enough. You are beloved. You are Mine."

This is the love that has the power to transform us. When we truly understand God's unconditional love, it changes everything. It frees us from the need for human approval, from the endless cycle of people-pleasing. It gives us the courage to be our true selves, not the version we think others want us to be. It brings us deep joy and peace, even in the midst of hard circumstances.

But how can we tap into this transformative love? How can we experience God's unconditional acceptance in our everyday lives?

Your True Worth

Here are a few practical steps:

- Spend time in His Word. The Bible is full of stories and truths that showcase God's deep love for us. Memorize verses that speak to your identity in Christ and let them sink deep into your soul.

- Pray with vulnerability. Don't be afraid to come to God as you are, with all your doubts and fears and insecurities. He can handle your honesty, and He meets you in your brokenness.

- Accept His forgiveness. When you mess up (and you will), don't wallow in guilt and shame. Instead, accept God's forgiveness, just as you would offer it to a friend. Let His grace cover you.

Your True Worth

- Listen for His whispers. In the quiet moments,
  God whispers truths of love and worth over you.
  Practice listening for His voice, letting His words
  be the ones that define you.

God's unconditional love has the power to change
everything. It's the antidote to the world's conditional
love, the balm to our souls. And it's available to us, right
now, just as we are.

Take a moment to reflect on where you're seeking
conditional love. Where are you trying to earn approval,
rather than accepting the unconditional love of God?
What steps can you take to tap into His transformative
love, and let it define you?

Chapter 6: Biblical Examples of Those Who Found Validation in God

"Am I now trying to win the approval of human beings, or of God? Or am I trying to please people? If I were still trying to please people, I would not be a servant of Christ." - Galatians 1:10

The Bible is full of examples of those who found validation in God, not in the approval of others.

Let's look at a few of these stories and see what we can learn from their journeys.

> **David:** Before he was king, David was just a shepherd boy, overlooked by his family and society. But God saw him, and God anointed him to lead His people. Even when Saul, the current

king, tried to kill him, David refused to take
matters into his own hands. Instead, he trusted in
God's validation, knowing that if God had called
him, that was all the approval he needed.

Esther: Esther was a Jewish girl who found
herself as queen of Persia, in a position to save
her people from genocide. But it was a dangerous
position – if she approached the king without
being summoned, she could be put to death. Still,
with the encouragement of her cousin Mordecai,
Esther chose to risk her life, trusting that if God
had placed her in this position, He would give her
the courage and favor she needed. She found
validation not in her royal status, but in her faith
in God's sovereignty.

Your True Worth

Paul: Before his conversion, Paul (then known as Saul) was a Pharisee, dedicated to persecuting the early Christians. But on the road to Damascus, he had an encounter with the risen Jesus that changed everything. Though he lost the approval of his peers, though he suffered greatly for his faith, Paul found a new validation in Christ. He became a servant of Jesus, pleasing God rather than people.

These stories, and many others like them in the Bible, teach us that when we find our validation in God, we're free to live a life pleasing to Him, not others. We're free to take risks, to stand up for what's right, to be who He created us to be, even if that means disappointing others. So how can we be like David, Esther, Paul, and the others who found validation in God?

Your True Worth

Here are a few practical steps:

- Seek God's approval above all else. In every decision, every action, ask yourself: Am I trying to please God, or am I trying to please people?

- Trust in God's sovereignty. Believe that if God has called you to something, He will equip you for it. His validation is all you need to move forward.

- Be willing to take risks. If God is leading you down a certain path, don't let fear of what others think hold you back. Step out in faith, trusting in His favor and protection.

- Find your identity in Christ. At the end of the day, it's not about your title, your status, your achievements. It's about being a beloved child of God. Let this truth be the one that defines you.

Your True Worth

When you find your validation in God, you're free to live the life He designed for you.

You're free to be who He created you to be, to do what He's called you to do, to bring Him glory in all things. And that's a life of true freedom and fulfillment.

Take a moment to reflect on where you're finding validation. Is it in God's eyes, or in the approval of others? What steps can you take to be like David, Esther, Paul, and the others who found validation in Him?

Chapter 7: The Power of Prayer and Meditation in Seeking God's Approval

"Seek first his kingdom and his righteousness, and all these things will be given to you as well." - Matthew 6:33

When we're seeking validation from the world, our focus is outward. We're constantly looking to others, trying to earn their approval and acceptance. But when we're seeking validation from God, our focus shifts inward. We turn our eyes upon Him, seeking His kingdom and His righteousness above all else.

This is where prayer and meditation come in. These practices help us quiet the noise of the world and tune into God's voice. They help us seek His approval, not by striving to earn it, but by simply being with Him.

Prayer: Prayer is how we communicate with God. It's how we pour out our hearts to Him, sharing our hopes and fears, our dreams and doubts. And it's how He communicates with us, whispering truths of love and worth deep into our souls. When we make prayer a priority, we're seeking God's approval in every moment. We're inviting Him into our lives, asking for His guidance and wisdom.

Meditation: Meditation is when we take a step beyond prayer, quieting ourselves to truly listen for God's voice. It's when we take a verse or a truth from His Word and soak in it, letting it sink deep into our hearts. In meditation, we're not striving to earn God's approval, but

Your True Worth

simply resting in His presence. We're reminding ourselves that we're already beloved, already enough, just as we are.

When we prioritize prayer and meditation, we're seeking God's kingdom and His righteousness. We're seeking His approval above all else. And when we do, He promises to give us everything we need. He'll guide us, provide for us, give us peace in the midst of chaos. He'll remind us that we're His, that we're enough, not because of what we've done, but because of who He is.

So how can you make prayer and meditation a priority in your life?

Here are a few practical steps:

Your True Worth

- Start small. Begin with just a few minutes of prayer and meditation each day. As you get into the habit, you can gradually increase your time.

- Find a quiet space. Get away from the noise of the world. Find a quiet spot where you can be alone with God.

- Be honest. In your prayers, be honest with God. Share your true feelings, your doubts and fears. He can handle it, and He meets you in your brokenness.

- Listen. In meditation, listen for God's voice. He may not speak in an audible way, but He'll whisper truths into your heart. Be still and listen.

When you make prayer and meditation a priority, you're seeking God's approval above all else. You're inviting Him into your life, asking for His guidance and wisdom.

Your True Worth

And He promises to meet you there, to give you all you need. He'll remind you that you're His, that you're enough, just as you are.

Take a moment to reflect on your current prayer and meditation practice. Where can you make room to seek God's approval in a more intentional way? What steps can you take to prioritize these practices, and invite God more fully into your life?

Chapter 8: Embracing Our Identity in Christ

"I praise you because I am fearfully and wonderfully made; your works are wonderful, I know that full well." - Psalm 139:14

When we're seeking validation from the world, our identity is always shifting. We're like a chameleon, changing to blend in with our surroundings. But this is exhausting, and it leaves us feeling lost and uncertain. Because the truth is, we can't find our true identity in the approval of others. We can only find it in the unconditional love of God.

When we embrace our identity in Christ, everything changes. We're no longer trying to earn love and

Your True Worth

acceptance, because we know we already have it. We're

no longer comparing ourselves to others, because we

know we're uniquely created with a purpose all our own.

We're no longer striving to be enough, because we know

we're enough just as we are.

So how can we embrace our identity in Christ?

Here are a few practical steps:

- Know God's Word. The Bible is full of truths
  about who we are in Christ. Spend time reading
  it, memorizing it, letting its words define you. •
  Reject lies. When the world (or your own inner
  critic) tells you you're not enough, reject those
  lies. Replace them with the truth of God's Word.
- Embrace your uniqueness. You're not like anyone
  else, and that's a good thing! Embrace the ways

Your True Worth

you're uniquely wired, the gifts and talents that make you, you.

- Live from a place of worth. You don't have to earn God's love, you already have it. Live from a place of worth, extending love and grace to yourself and others.

When you embrace your identity in Christ, you're free to be who He created you to be. You're free to live the life He designed for you, to bring Him glory in all things. And that's a life of true freedom and fulfillment.

Take a moment to reflect on where you're finding your identity. Is it in the world's approval, or in God's unconditional love? What steps can you take to embrace your true identity in Christ, and live from a place of worth?

Part 3

Living a Life Freed from the Need for

Human Approval

Chapter 9: Courage to Make Decisions Aligned with Faith, Not Opinion

"It is for freedom that Christ has set us free. Stand firm, then, and do not let yourselves be burdened again by a yoke of slavery." - Galatians 5:1

When we're seeking validation from the world, our decisions are often driven by the opinions of others. We say yes to things we don't really want to do, not wanting to disappoint others. We stay in situations that are draining or toxic, afraid of what others will think if we leave. We're like a leaf blown by the wind, constantly shifting direction based on the whims of those around us.

But this is not the freedom that Christ offers us. When we're rooted in His unconditional love and acceptance,

Your True Worth

we have the courage to make decisions that align with

our faith, not just the opinions of others. We're no longer

slaves to what others think, but instead, we're free to

follow God's leading, even if that means going against

the crowd.

So how can we make decisions that are aligned with our

faith, not just the opinions of others?

Here are a few practical steps:

- Seek God's guidance. Before making a decision,

  take time to pray and seek God's wisdom. Ask for

  His guidance and direction. Pour out your heart

  to Him, and listen for His still, small voice.

- Listen to your intuition. God often speaks to us

  through our intuition. Pay attention to that gut

feeling, that sense of peace or unease. It may be the Holy Spirit guiding you.

- Be willing to say no. Just as important as knowing what to say yes to is knowing what to say no to. Don't be afraid to set boundaries, to decline opportunities that don't align with your values or goals. Your time and energy are finite – invest them in the things that truly matter.

- Don't seek validation for every decision. You don't need everyone's approval for every choice you make. Seek counsel from trusted advisors, but don't be afraid to make decisions without consensus. Sometimes, the most faithful decision is the unpopular one.

When we make decisions that are aligned with our faith, we're living in the freedom that Christ offers us. We're

Your True Worth

not burdened by the opinions of others, but instead, we're free to follow God's leading. And that's a life of true freedom and fulfillment.

Take a moment to reflect on your decision-making process. Are you making decisions based on your faith, or are you seeking the validation of others? What steps can you take to seek God's guidance and live in the freedom He offers?

Chapter 10: Finding Confidence in God's Purpose for Our Lives

"For I know the plans I have for you," declares the Lord, "plans to prosper you and not to harm you, plans to give you hope and a future." - Jeremiah 29:11

When we're seeking validation from the world, we're often looking for confidence in all the wrong places. We think that if we can just achieve this one thing, or get approval from that person, we'll finally feel good enough. But the truth is, our confidence will always be shaky when it's built on the shifting sands of human opinion.

True confidence comes from knowing God's purpose for our lives and living in alignment with it. When we

Your True Worth

understand that we're uniquely created with gifts and talents to bring Him glory, we can walk in the confidence that comes from knowing we're exactly where we're meant to be.

So how can we find confidence in God's purpose for our lives?

Here are a few practical steps:

- Seek God's vision. Spend time in prayer, asking God to reveal His vision for your life. What passions has He put in your heart? What problems is He calling you to solve?
- Identify your gifts. What are you naturally good at? Where do you feel most alive? These clues can point to God's purpose for you.

Your True Worth

- Take small steps. Once you have a sense of God's purpose, don't feel like you have to have it all figured out. Take small steps towards the vision, and trust God to guide you as you go.

- Embrace the journey. Finding and living out God's purpose isn't always a linear path. There will be twists and turns, ups and downs. Embrace the journey, trusting that God is always working things out for your good.

When you find your confidence in God's purpose, you'll walk in a freedom and boldness that's unshakeable. You'll be able to take risks, to step into the unknown, to be the person God created you to be. And that's a life of true fulfillment and purpose.

Your True Worth

Take a moment to reflect on where you're seeking

confidence. Is it in the world's approval, or in God's

purpose for your life? What steps can you take to seek

His vision, and live in the confidence that comes from

knowing you're exactly where you're meant to be?

Chapter 11: Healthy Relationships Built on God's Love

"Love is patient, love is kind. It does not envy, it does not boast, it is not proud. It does not dishonor others, it is not self-seeking, it is not easily angered, it keeps no record of wrongs. Love does not delight in evil but rejoices with the truth. It always protects, always trusts, always hopes, always perseveres." - 1 Corinthians 13:4-7

When we're seeking validation from the world, our relationships can become imbalanced. We may find ourselves people-pleasing, constantly trying to earn the approval of others. Or we may become approval-addicts, constantly seeking the validation of others to feel good enough. But these patterns lead to unhealthy relationships, ones that are draining and unsatisfying.

Your True Worth

But when we're rooted in God's unconditional love, we can build healthy, life-giving relationships. We're not looking to others to complete us, because we know we're already whole in Christ. We're free to love others without expectation of return, to serve without needing approval. We're able to set boundaries, to communicate openly and honestly. We're able to forgive freely, without keeping a record of wrongs.

So how can we build healthy relationships rooted in God's love?

Here are a few practical steps:

- Know your worth. Before you can have healthy relationships with others, you need to know your own worth. Spend time in God's Word, letting His truths define you.

Your True Worth

- Practice self-care. Take care of yourself physically, emotionally, spiritually. This will give you the energy to love others well.

- Communicate openly. Don't assume others can read your mind. Communicate your needs and feelings in a clear, respectful way.

- Set boundaries. It's okay to say no. Set boundaries that protect your time and energy and communicate them clearly.

- Forgive freely. Holding onto resentment drains your energy. Practice forgiveness, not for others' sake, but for yours.

When you build your relationships on the foundation of God's love, you'll experience the kind of community and connection that brings joy and fulfillment. You'll be able

Your True Worth

to love and be loved, to give and receive, to be who God

created you to be. And that's a life of true abundance.

Take a moment to reflect on your relationships. Are they

built on the foundation of God's love, or are you seeking

validation from others? What steps can you take to build

healthier, more life-giving relationships?

Chapter 12: Sharing the Freedom Found in God's Validation with Others

"Praise be to the God and Father of our Lord Jesus Christ, the Father of compassion and the God of all comfort, who comforts us in all our troubles, so that we can comfort those in any trouble with the comfort we ourselves received from God." - 2 Corinthians 1:3-4

When we've experienced the freedom that comes from seeking God's validation, we can't help but want to share it with others. We've tasted the sweetness of His unconditional love, and we long for those around us to experience it too.

So how can we share this freedom with others?

Here are a few practical steps:

Your True Worth

- Be vulnerable. Share your own story of seeking validation from the world, and how you found freedom in God's love. Your vulnerability can help others feel less alone.

- Extend grace. Just as God has extended grace to you, extend it to others. Don't expect perfection, but instead, offer understanding and compassion.

- Speak truth. When others are seeking validation from the world, gently point them to the truth of God's Word. Remind them of their worth in His eyes. • Listen well. Sometimes, the most powerful thing we can do is simply listen. Create space for others to share their hearts and listen without judgment.

Your True Worth

- Pray with others. Prayer is a powerful way to invite God into a situation. Pray with others, asking for His guidance, comfort, and wisdom.

When we share the freedom we've found in God's validation, we get to be part of His redemptive story. We get to help others experience the same unconditional love that has transformed our lives. And that's a life of true purpose and fulfillment.

Take a moment to reflect on who you could share this freedom with. Is there a friend, family member, or colleague who is seeking validation from the world? What steps can you take to point them to the unconditional love of God?

Conclusion

As we come to the end of this book, I want to leave you
with a final blessing and a burning challenge. May you
feel, deep in the marrow of your bones, the unconditional
love of God. May His validation be the North Star that
guides you, the anchor that holds you fast, the safe
harbor where you always find peace. May you walk in
the freedom and favor that flows from being a beloved
child of God, and may your life shine like a beacon,
reflecting His glory to all.

Remember, the journey of seeking God's validation is
not a destination – it's a lifelong adventure. There will be
mountaintops and valleys, detours, and dead ends. But
through it all, God is your constant companion, your
faithful guide, your unwavering cheerleader. Don't just

Your True Worth

peep at the world through the bars of others'
expectations. Break free, spread your wings, and soar
into the person He created you to be. Find your
confidence in His purpose and watch as you dance in the
downpour of His freedom and favor.

This is the life God designed for you – a masterpiece of
freedom and fulfillment, of purpose and joy that
overflows like a fountain. A life that brings Him glory in
every step, every breath, every moment. So go and live
it, unapologetically and boldly. The world is starving for
the person God made you to be.

And when the road gets rocky, and doubts howl like
wolves at the door, come back to this unshakeable truth:
You are enough. You are beloved. You are God's, now

Your True Worth

and forever. And His validation is the only applause that
truly matters.

With blessings on your journey,

Sweeden

A Prayer for the Journey Ahead

Dear Heavenly Father,

As we close this book and embark on the journey ahead, we come before you with open hearts and open hands. We surrender to you, Lord – our fears and doubts, our dreams and desires. We ask that you fill us with your Spirit, that you would guide us and equip us for the path you have set before us.

Help us to seek your validation above all else, to find our confidence in your purpose for our lives. Give us the courage to be who you created us to be, and to walk in the freedom and favor that comes from being your beloved children.

Your True Worth

Bring into our lives the people you have appointed to support and encourage us so that we might live in a community and connection that brings joy and fulfillment. Use us, Lord, to bring you glory in all things, that we might be lights in the darkness and reflections of your love.

When the road gets rough and doubts creep in, anchor us in the truth of your unconditional love. Remind us that we are enough, that we are beloved, that we are yours. Let your validation be the applause we seek, the approval we crave.

We thank you, Lord, for the life you have designed for us – a life of true freedom and fulfillment, of purpose and joy that overflows. Help us to live it,

Your True Worth

unapologetically and boldly, so that the world might see

you in us and know your love.

In the name of Jesus, we pray. Amen.

Your True Worth

Your True Worth

Your True Worth

c65277b8-40af-418d-ac5f-35ca6d9ca232R01